Coin Collecting Guide

A Beginner's Guide to the Basics of Coin Collecting so That You Can Start Your Own Rare Coin Collection as a Hobby or Make a Profit by Recognizing and Selling the Right Coins

By Charlie Wilderman

© **Copyright 2019 - All rights reserved.**

The content contained within this book may not be reproduced, duplicated or transmitted without direct written permission from the author or the publisher.

Under no circumstances will any blame or legal responsibility be held against the publisher or author for any damages, reparation, or monetary loss due to the information contained within this book. Either directly or indirectly.

Legal Notice:

This book is copyright protected. This book is only for personal use. You cannot amend, distribute, sell, use, quote or paraphrase any part, or the content within this book, without the consent of the author or publisher.

Disclaimer Notice:

Please note the information contained within this document is for educational and entertainment purposes only. All effort has been executed to present accurate, up to date and reliable, complete information. No warranties of any kind are declared or implied. Readers acknowledge that the author is not engaging in the rendering of legal, financial, medical or professional advice. The content within this book has been derived from various sources. Please consult a licensed professional before attempting any techniques outlined in this book.

By reading this document, the reader agrees that under no

circumstances is the author responsible for any losses, direct or indirect, which are incurred as a result of the use of information contained within this document, including, but not limited to, —errors, omissions, or inaccuracies.

Contents

Introduction 1

Chapter 1: Some Exciting Facts About Coins 3

Chapter 2: Coin Collecting Glossary 9

    Alloy 9

    Ancient 9

    Bag marks 9

    Bi-metallic Coin 9

    Blank 10

    Bullion 10

    Cameo 10

    Circulated Coin 10

    Commemorative Coin 10

    Error Coin 11

    Grade 11

    High Points 11

    Legend 11

    Mintage 12

    Mint Mark 12

    Mint State 12

    Numismatics 12

    Obverse 12

    Proof coins 13

    Reverse 13

    Rim 13

Un-circulated Coin. 13

Variety 13

Chapter 3: Starting Your Collection 15

Chapter 4: What To Collect 18

Chapter 5: Saving Your Coins 26

Chapter 6: Tools Of The Trade 27

Accumulating Your Collection 30

Chapter 7: Managing Your Coins 33

Chapter 8: Cleaning up Coins 35

Chapter 9: Grading Your Coins 39

Mint State Perfect Uncirculated (MS-70). 39

Choice Uncirculated (MS-65). 40

Un-circulated (MS-60). 40

Choice About Uncirculated (AU-55) 40

About Un-circulated (AU-50). 40

Extremely Fine (EF-40). 41

Very Fine (VF-20). 41

Fine (F-12). 41

Very Good (VG-8). 41

Good (G-4). 42

About Good (AG-3). 42

Chapter 10: Figuring Out Your Coin's Value 43

Chapter 11: Pricing Coins 46

Chapter 12: The Majority Of Requested Coin Values 48

Circulated U.S. Wheat Cents (1958 and earlier) 48

1943 "Steel Cents" 48

Silver Dimes, Quarters and Halves 49

Silver Dollars 50

Susan B. Anthony Dollars 50

Bicentennial Quarters, Halves and Dollars 51

Coin Honoring the Wedding Event of Prince Charles and Princess Diana 51

A Coin with 2 Heads, 2 Tails or Mules 51

An Un-struck Coin 53

A "Mis-struck" Coin 53

Chapter 13: Pricey Coins 54

Chapter 14: Kids And Coin Collecting 57

They Can Boost Their Reading Capability 57

It is Going to Boost Their Understanding 57

They Can Refine Their Organizational Abilities 58

They Establish an Interest in History and Culture 58

The Capability to Set and Reach Goals 58

It Develops Self-confidence. 59

They are Going to Need to Develop Priorities 59

Value 59

Getting A Kid Started 60

Conclusion 62

Thank you for buying this book and I hope that you will find it useful. If you will want to share your thoughts on this book, you can do so by leaving a review on the Amazon page, it helps me out a lot.

Introduction

" Money makes the world go 'round." We constantly desire more of it, it commences wars, it purchases liberty, and for some, it's a great pastime. For coin collectors, cash is far more than a piece of metal or paper. It's a pastime, an understanding experience, and a long-lasting fixation.

There are no hard stats on the number of individuals who gather coins, however it's been approximated that 1 out of every 10,000 folks is a devoted coin collector.

Individuals have actually been collecting coins for quite a while. At one time, it was referred to as the hobby of kings, however today individuals from all walks of life and of all ages are keeping coin collections.

Their reasons are varied. Some enjoy the history at the bottom of coinage. Some do it to accumulate a collection deserving of handing down to upcoming generations. Still, others are just business folks purchasing and selling coins to earn a living. Collecting coins could be somewhat of a treasure hunt. The mission for that one coin to finalize a collection can be a fixation.

The practice of numismatics, the collection and analyzing of coins, paper currency, tokens and medals, provides the collector with various areas to focus on.

Chapter 1: Some Exciting Facts About Coins

There are roughly $8 billion worth of coins flowing in the U.S. today. Over the last 30 years, the U.S. Mint, who is in charge of creating and producing the country's coins, has actually minted over 300 billion coins, worth about $15 billion.

Ever since its conception in 1792, the U.S. Mint has turned into a big business with more than $1 billion in yearly earnings and 2,200 workers. It is, without a doubt the world's biggest producer of coins and medals, producing coins not just for the U.S. yet on behalf of numerous other nations too.

To create coins, the U.S. Mint buys strips of metal (rolled into coils) in the appropriate measurements and density.

Zinc metal strips covered with copper plating are utilized to make cents. Strips utilized for nickels are made up of 75% copper, 25% nickel metal alloy. Dimes, quarters, half-dollars and dollar coins are made of strips being composed of 3 metal layers merged together. The external layers of these strips are made up of the very same alloy as that utilized for nickels with the third (core) layer being made up of copper.

The initial step in the coin making procedure includes feeding the metal strips through a "blanking" press. The press punches out cut round discs, or blanks, about the identical size as the completed coin. These blanks are after that, warmed up in a furnace to soften them. Consequently, the softened blanks are put in turning barrels of chemical solutions to clean and refine the metal. The cleaned up and glossy blanks are then cleaned and dried.

Subsequently, the blanks are arranged to get rid of any malfunctioning ones and the rest are put through an "upsetting" mill which raises a rim across their edges. The rimmed blanks after that head to the coining or marking press where upper and lower dies stamp the designs and engravings on both sides of the coin all at once. At this moment, the blanks end up being real U.S. coins.

Lastly, the completed coins are mechanically counted and put into big canvas bags for delivery to the Federal Reserve Banks. From there, they are delivered to regional banks on an as-needed basis.

When the U. S. Mint was created, the law required that all coins be crafted from gold, silver or copper. For a substantial time period later on, gold was utilized in the $10, $5 and $2.50 pieces, silver was utilized to create the dollar, half-dollar, quarter, dime and half-dime while the cent and half-cent coins were crafted from copper.

In 1933, throughout the Great Depression, the U.S. Mint stopped producing gold coins completely. In 1965, due to an extreme silver lack, Congress dictated that silver no longer be utilized in creating quarters and dimes. Additionally, the silver material of the half-dollar (formerly 90%) was lowered to 40% in 1965 and after that, removed completely in 1971.

All of these coin denominations are now comprised of copper-nickel dressed with an external layer of a 75% copper, 25% nickel alloy and a pristine copper core. Nickels are composed of the identical copper-nickel alloy yet without the copper core.

The cent's structure was modified in 1982 from 95% copper 5% zinc, to the present 97.5% zinc, 2.5% copper mix. This was done as a cost-cutting step and to make the cent lighter in weight.

The quarter, dime, nickel and cent are the coin denominations typically in use today. The half-dollar and dollar coins are released, however hardly ever flow in daily commerce. Foreign coins exist in all kinds of denominations, so it's difficult to note them all here.

U.S. coin denominations released in the past, but no more in use consist of the half-cent, two-cent, three-cent, and 20-cent copper bits and a little silver coin called a half-dime. Gold coins in denominations of $1, $2.50 ("Quarter Eagle"), $3, $5 ("Half Eagle"), $10 ("Eagle"), and $20 ("Double Eagle") were issued from time to time from 1793 up until 1933.

Silver half-dollars have actually been minted in big numbers since 1793 and culminated in popularity with the arrival of the Kennedy half-dollar in 1964. Silver-less half-dollars were initially presented in 1971.

Silver dollars have actually been released at different times since 1793, were terminated in 1933, and after that reintroduced in 1971 in the form of the silver-less Eisenhower dollar. The Eisenhower dollar was substituted in 1979 with the silver less Susan B. Anthony coin, in respect of the renowned women's suffrage pioneer.

A brand-new dollar coin substituted the Susan B. Anthony coins. That coin depicts Sacagawea, the Native American woman who brought about the prosperity of the Lewis and Clark expedition. The coin is a gold color and created from a manganese brass metal alloy.

Additionally, "commemorative" coins have actually been released from time to time in different denominations to commemorate a specific notable individual, location or occasion. These coins are typically made in minimal amounts, sell at a premium and hardly ever circulate as typical coinage. The initial such coin was released in 1892 to honor the World Columbian Exposition in Chicago.

With the exception of commemorative coins and the Susan B. Anthony dollar, U.S. coins presently depict previous Presidents. These coins are the Lincoln penny, presented in 1909, the Washington quarter, initially released in 1932, the Jefferson nickel, embraced in 1938, the Franklin D. Roosevelt dime, presented in 1946, and the Kennedy half-dollar, which was initially minted in 1964.

In 1792, Congress demanded that all American coins reveal on one side "an impression emblematic of Freedom, with the engraving of Freedom, and the year of coinage."

The expression "In God We Trust" was initially utilized on U.S. coins in 1864. This slogan now shows up on all U.S. coins.

In 1999, the design of the U.S. quarter altered. Reverses of flowing quarters will be substituted with designs symbolical of each of the fifty states. Every year from 1999 through 2008, five various quarters, honoring 5 states will be released in the order by which the states ratified the Constitution or were admitted to the Union. These "State Quarters" are meant for general flow; however, exclusive silver proof coins are going to additionally be offered to collectors.

The coins of other countries can show several images involving animals, scenes, popular buildings, and more. They frequently show the history of the country and are intriguing for the newbie collector because of their originality.

The initial worldwide convention for coin collectors was held in August of 1962 in Detroit, Michigan. It was funded by the American Numismatic Association and the Canadian numismatic Association. It was approximated that over 40,000 individuals participated in this initial convention.

Chapter 2: Coin Collecting Glossary

Coin collecting has its own unique terms or "terminology." The following, while not an extensive list of all the coin collecting terms that you might experience, offers definitions for the most frequently utilized terms.

Alloy

A mix of 2 or more metals in a coin like cupro-nickel or cupro-zinc.

Ancient

Describes any coin minted prior to 500 A.D.

Bag marks

Nicks, marks and scratches arising from coins in a mint bag touching with one another.

Bi-metallic Coin

A coin with the center created from one metal with its external part being made up of various metals.

Blank

A round piece of metal created for future minting into coinage.

Bullion

A coin crafted from gold or additional precious metal with little numismatic worth aside from the existing value of the metal from which the coin is created.

Cameo

A coin with a frosted look.

Circulated Coin

A coin which has, in fact, been utilized as cash and shows some level of wear.

Commemorative Coin

A coin with a layout struck in tribute of some historic or present occasion, famous individual or a particular anniversary.

Error Coin

A coin minted accidentally or with a design different than planned.

Grade

The status of a coin identified by a set methodology.

High Points

The highest part of a coin's design where the initial indications of deterioration usually show up.

Legend

The words that are engraved around the external edge of a coin, for U.S. coins, the legend engraving is E Pluribus Unum.

Mintage

The total number of coins of a specific denomination, date and/or kind created by a mint.

Mint Mark

A sign pinpointing the specific mint which created the coin.

Mint State

An un-circulated coin in the identical condition as when it was initially minted revealing no indications of damage.

Numismatics

The study of coins, paper money, tokens, medals, and other comparable objects.

Obverse

The "heads" side of the coin where a picture of a president, king, queen or other national leader shows up.

Proof coins

Coins that are struck with more substantial pressure than typical utilizing particularly polished dies to make the style more strongly refined or mirror-like.

Reverse

The back or "tails" part of a coin, the opposite side to the obverse side of a coin.

Rim

The external edge of a coin.

Un-circulated Coin.

A coin that has actually never really been utilized as cash and has no noticeable indications of damage.

Variety

Any modification in the design of a coin leads to a brand-new coin variety.

There are more terms which we are going to attempt to describe as they show up within this book, however, this is a great start for the starting collector.

Chapter 3: Starting Your Collection

There are a couple of individuals who do have at least the start of a coin collection. A number of us possess at least one or more "good luck coins," a big cent, an old Indian nickel or silver dollar, a medal or a memento token. Any one of these objects has actually frequently resulted in the beginning of a big coin collection and a brand-new pastime.

Coins are interesting due to the fact that they frequently show stories of royalty, terrific leaders, history, power and patriotism relating to their particular nations of issuance. Famous figures materialize when portrayed on an old coin. For instance, Julius Caesar and Alexander the Great, in ancient times; Henry VIII, Napoleon, George Washington and Abraham Lincoln are all shown on coins exactly as they appeared back then.

It's ideal to begin your collection by picking what you wish to collect. It's challenging to state, "I simply wish to collect coins" due to the fact that there are hundreds and hundreds and hundreds to pick from. If you wish to simply accumulate a couple of stray coins for your own enjoyment, by all means, do so. However, this is not actually coin collecting.

Real collectors aim to complete sets of coins. That's part of the appeal, searching for coins that are going to suit their set. Do not attempt to focus on way too many classifications as it can end up being lengthy and costly. You might wish to participate in a coin show to see a few of the specialized collections frequently on display and discover one that interests you.

It is necessary to research the pastime, a lot. This book is an excellent start, however there are numerous other publications to acquaint yourself with. If you do not research the pastime, you run the risk of investing a great deal of cash on over-priced and counterfeit coins.

Collecting coins from circulation is a terrific location to begin. The risk is minimal (you can constantly spend the coins), and you are able to find out a lot analyzing your coins thoroughly and seeing what a reference book states about them.

This is the simplest and least costly method to start collecting coins. You should do it methodically, however. Or else, you are going to let way too many great coins get away. Each day, set aside any coins you get in change. Keep them either in a different pocket or in a different area inside your bag. Do this with each coin you get.

Then, at night, look at the change, keeping the coins you do not have. Additionally, compare your day's catch with the coins within your collection, and exchange the inferior coins in your collection for greater ones from the change. By regularly inspecting your change daily, you not only contribute to your collection, yet you additionally improve its condition. Improving a coin is nearly as enjoyable as discovering it.

Chapter 4: What To Collect

What to collect is completely up to the collector. It is going to generally be a specialization that holds some interest for the collector and is inside his/her budget.

Amongst the most prominent kinds of collections are world coins (coins from numerous nations), ancient coins, and coins of a specific nation. Some specialization within these classifications is generally valuable. If collecting from a specific nation, you can deal with several series, a type set, commemoratives, errors, die varieties, paper currency, and so on. You might likewise wish to set bounds on the grades of coins you gather, e.g. all G-VG, VF or better, or uncirculated.

You might collect a whole series. The objective of a series collector is to obtain one of each date and mintmark made, typically consisting of any significant design distinctions. For instance, the U.S. Standing Liberty quarter was created from 1916 to 1930 at the Philadelphia, Denver and San Francisco mints (coins were not created at all three mints each year, and none were created at any mint in 1922); a significant modification to the obverse was made in 1917, and the complete set is typically considered to incorporate both designs for that year from every mint.

A collector establishing a type set aims to possess one of each series and significant design variation in each series. Instances would be 20th century Canadian coinage or U.S. gold coins.

You might select to concentrate on ancient coins. That is, coins that were minted before 500 A.D. A lot of these remain in a theme and that is one method to concentrate your collection. Specialists claim that the gold, bronze, and silver coins of the ancient world are, in fact, rather readily available today and are less costly than you would expect.

Tokens are likewise prominent with collectors. When the government overlooked the requirements of individuals and declined to release enough low-value coins, the traders took concerns into their own hands and released tokens. In Great Britain, this happened in the mid-1600s, the 1790s and the 1810s. They formed a regional currency and it took numerous acts of Parliament to prohibit them. The bans were never ever totally effective and 'advertising tickets' continued to be released through the mid-1800s. These were easily the identical size as farthings, the coin still in really short supply.

By the conclusion of Queen Victoria's reign, the requirement for tokens had actually gone, however there were all kinds of other comparable pieces being utilized. Bars gave out checks but since they were such a regular occurrence, no one thought to record how they were utilized.

The co-operative societies utilized checks to record the valuation of purchases made so that the appropriate quantity of dividend might be paid. Fruit pickers got tallies depending upon the amount of fruit picked. The most recent usage of tokens remains in video gaming and vending machines, as well as in public transportation.

Although less worthwhile than coins, tokens are, regardless, a lot more fascinating if you have an interest in regional history and like to perform research.

You might wish to check out collecting proof sets. Proof coins are specifically produced for sale at a premium to collectors and in some cases for exhibition or for presentation as a present or award. Proofs are usually discernible from regular coins by their mirror-like fields, frosty devices (specifically over the last few years) and additional sharp details.

To acquire these qualities, each proof coin die is refined to produce an incredibly smooth surface and utilized for a limited amount of coins. Planchets are hand-fed to the coin press, where they are struck at a higher than normal pressure. Struck coins are extracted by hand with gloves or tongs. Contemporary proof coins are typically packaged in clear plastic to shield them from handling, wetness, and so on. For numerous years the U.S. Mint has actually offered yearly sets of proof coins. These "routine" proof sets typically include one proof coin of each denomination minted. In

1983, 1984 and 1986-97, Prestige Sets were likewise offered. Prestige Sets consist of all the coins in the routine set, plus a couple of commemorative coins released the very same year.

Since 1992, the Mint has actually additionally provided Silver Proof Sets, that include 90% silver variations of the proof dime, quarter(s) and a half dollar.

From 1992 through 1998, the Mint additionally offered a Premier Silver Proof Set. The two kinds of silver proof sets consist of the identical coins, with the premier set housing them in nicer looking wrapping.

You might additionally collect slabs. A licensed coin, or slab, is a coin that has actually been verified, graded and framed in a sonically sealed, tough plastic holder by an expert accreditation service. The holder affords protection from subsequent damage or deterioration but is not airtight and for that reason will not protect against toning. Since any tampering with the holder is going to be apparent, it likewise prevents substituting the licensed coin with something else.

Fake and modified coins slabbed by significant accreditation services are not unknown but are uncommon. The genuineness of a coin might be ensured by the provider that slabbed it. For that reason, a coin slabbed by a notable accreditation service provides some protection, specifically when counterfeits are understood to exist and the potential purchaser is unable to determine its legitimacy dependably.

As we are going to go over later on, grades are opinions. The identical coin might get various grades if submitted to various services and even if "cracked out" and resubmitted to the identical service. Additionally, grading requirements for some uncirculated coins have actually altered because slabs were initially produced (1986), so a coin in an early slab might get a different grade if resubmitted today.

The grade showed on a slab stands for the opinions of a couple of individuals who took a look at the coin when it was submitted. Therefore, slabbed coins given similar grades might have different market values. When possible, purchase the coin, not the holder.

Prices vary from $7.50 to $175.00 per coin, depending upon the service and turn-around time, plus delivery fees in both directions.

The abilities and tools required to encapsulate coins in slab-like holders can be obtained more quickly than the knowledge required to precisely validate and grade coins. Holders from the services noted above are not the only kinds that show up in the market.

Nevertheless, slabs from some "services" might not be regarded by knowledgeable numismatists as genuine and might not even be backed by a warranty of the coin's genuineness. Finding out about the service's track record and obtaining other viewpoints about a coin's condition might spare you from paying substantially more than its real market value.

Some collectors focus on world coins. This is the phrase provided to collections of fairly recent contemporary coins from countries around the globe. Collectors of world coins are typically curious about geography. They are able to "travel the world" vicariously via their collecting.

A popular method to gather world coins is to get representative examples from each nation or coin issuing authority. Some collect by topic. This might be discovering coins from around the globe that present animals.

Since world coins are generally really affordable, this might be a great beginning point for kids. Lots of kids discover foreign coins by looking under change-to-cash machines where customers throw away various coins discovered in their penny jars. A few of these could be from Canada, South Africa, or Mexico.

Here are some other recommendations on methods to classify your coin collection and concentrate your efforts.

23

- Collect coins from a particular nation or group of nations.

- A collector by kind or series intends to get one of each kind or series of coins, for instance, U.S. eagles or Lincoln cents.

- You might want to focus on coins made from a specific metal like silver or gold coins.

- Think about collecting coins with a specific style like coins with animal styles, boat styles or numerous commemorative coins like Olympic coins.

- Some collectors concentrate on coins issued with some mistake in the coin's layout, structure, date or engraving.

- One more specialty is the collection of non-monetary "coins" like war medals and commemorative tokens.

- Save a cent, nickel, dime, and quarter from the year you were born. Search for one from every mint. Coins from the Denver Mint in Colorado and the Philadelphia Mint in Pennsylvania are distinct.

- Establish a coin set from each year since you were born. Look for them from both mints.

- Discover coins from around the globe. Find their nations on the map. Discover what the coins' pictures suggest to that nation.

Chapter 5: Saving Your Coins

Boxes, containers and bags might be utilized to save less important coins but are not usually enough for more worthwhile coins. There are specifically made coin envelopes created from acid-free paper that holds specific coins and offers an appropriate, affordable method to stash most coins.

Plastic resealable bags or "flips" are an excellent storage option, since they allow you to see the coin without taking it out from the cover. Mylar-lined cardboard sleeves (typically 2" x2") resemble plastic flips and are a great way to keep and bundle coins for delivery. Cardboard or plastic coin albums are fantastic for stashing a series of coins associated with a specific nation or motif.

Tubes are plastic containers that benefit keeping a number of low-cost coins of the identical size together. Extremely important coins are frequently "slabbed" or framed in tough plastic holders as this provides the greatest protection of any storage approach.

A number of things to bear in mind with storage: If you reside in a really damp location, add some silica gel to your storage container and maintain your coins in their storage containers in a protected location like a safe or fire-resistant box.

Chapter 6: Tools Of The Trade

There's very little you actually require to collect coins, aside from the coins. Since you might be dealing with precious coins, you must have a couple of particular items to protect their soundness.

You are going to require a magnifying glass to pick out the detail on your coins. All kinds of magnifiers are offered. For grading, 4-10 times zoom suffices, with 7x zoom considered by many to be perfect. Collectors of die varieties require 10x zoom or more.

You are going to additionally require a reference book to recognize your coins and evaluate their worth. Anybody buying coins must own at least one basic reference book with information on dates and mintmarks, significant varieties, grading standards and prices.

Extra references analyzing subjects in more detail (e.g. grading, fake detection or die varieties) are frequently helpful. Periodicals are going to have more recent pricing data and news. Great reference works can pay for themselves a number of times over by assisting you to stay away from bad choices.

Specialists take into consideration the five references listed below as the leading ones in the market. You might wish to choose one of these:

1) Red Book" - A Guide Book of United States Coins

This is the conventional brochure of market prices for U.S. coins featuring colonial issues. The prices are the most a collector may be expected to pay a vendor for a specific coin. This publication has a plethora of information about coin collecting. Each collector ought to own a copy. It is released yearly.

2) Coin Collectors Survival Manual

This book supplies numerous intriguing insights into coin collecting from the viewpoint of a knowledgeable coin dealer. Lots of coin collecting subjects are covered in an amusing manner.

3) Standard Catalog of World Coins

This catalog supplies values for 20th century world coins. This is a really extensive source of information on world coins.

4) Blue Book - Handbook of United States Coins

This book offers common prices that dealers are going to shell out for coins, in a specific grade or condition, from collectors or other dealers. It is released yearly too.

5) A Basic Guide to United States Commemorative Coins

This is a guide to the recognition and values of U.S. Commemorative Coins with pictures.

You might additionally wish to get an array of coin holders such as envelopes, fold & staple holders, coin folders and coin flips. For better coins, you may consider a few of the better-priced plastic holders which are offered for single coins and sets.

Coin Folders are often described as coin boards by the old-time collectors, and are the most affordable method to put together a series of coins into a set. Coin folders work effectively for a lower price and circulated coins. They're likewise terrific for children in addition to novices only beginning to collect coins.

If you select coin pages to show your collection, select quality vinyl pages with a lot of slots for your coins. The majority of coin pages are going to fit in a standard three-ring binder.

As you end up being a more skilled collector, you are going to most likely discover more supplies that are going to make your task less troublesome like a coin gauge and material to maintain your collection.

Accumulating Your Collection

The simplest method to begin collecting coins is to concentrate on the ones that are still in circulation. You might, nevertheless, wish to branch off into out of circulation coins.

Dealers with their personal coin stores can be excellent resources for information along with coins.

Participate in some coin shows. You can purchase from numerous dealers at the same time. The choice will undoubtedly be better than at most stores, and you might have the ability to get better prices.

Coins can be bought from lots of dealers through the mail. Sadly, it is all too common to get over-graded or problem coins from some mail-order sources. Make certain the source has a sensible return policy prior to buying. Analyze the coins thoroughly when you get them to guarantee they're acceptable. Get a viewpoint from a more skilled collector/dealer if you are uncertain, and return them in case they are not the quality you were counting on.

You can additionally have a go at auctions. This is going to consist of live auctions in addition to those carried out online like on e-bay.

The rarest and most costly coins are frequently offered just at auctions, promoted by significant specialized auction companies. These are normally in bigger cities.

It is not unusual for bids in these auctions to go substantially higher or lower than prices for similar coins from other sources. Check prices in stores, mail order advertisements or websites and restrict your bids to those prices to avoid paying an excessive amount.

Fairly typical collector coins are often featured in auctions of antiques, other collectibles, and estate auctions. Typically, the coins are over-graded, have issues not pointed out by the auctioneer, or come with inflated prices.

You are able to trade or purchase from another collector, but, it's challenging to find other collectors offering precisely what you desire. When it occurs, you might get a more desirable price.

There are additionally coin collector message boards you can utilize to make contacts. Simply take a look around or Google and you'll discover them.

Coins are often offered at flea markets, antique shows, craft fairs and other occasions where they are not the main focal point. Since there is little if any competition for the seller and numerous prospective purchasers are not well educated about the hobby, these places can be utilized to move problem coins and prices might be pumped up. While the collector constantly wants to be able to assess the quality of possible purchases and fairness of their prices, additional care is required in these circumstances.

Chapter 7: Managing Your Coins

In general, collectible coins must be managed thoroughly to prevent the possibility of causing damage or introducing compounds that might result in spots or color changes. Numerous holders are going to offer sufficient protection for common handling, however prior to removing a coin from its holder, think about whether it's truly required.

Never ever touch an un-circulated or proof coin anywhere but the edge. Finger prints alone might lower the coin's grade and, subsequently, its worth. Handling on the edge is necessary when analyzing another individual's coins, despite the grade. Get in the routine of picking up collectible coins by their edges, and it is going to quickly end up being automatic.

Avoid holding numismatic objects in front of your mouth. Little particles of wetness might ultimately trigger spots.

When placing a coin down outside of a holder, put it on a tidy, soft surface. A velvet pad is a perfect surface and vital for the routine handling of important material. A tidy soft fabric or tidy piece of blank paper might suffice for less valuable objects. Do not drag coins over any surfaces.

If you are going to be managing really important coins or a great deal of uncirculated or higher grade circulated coins, using tidy white fabric or surgical gloves and a mask might be a good idea.

Chapter 8: Cleaning up Coins

For the most part, you should not clean coins. While you may believe they'll appear nicer if they are glossy, collectors choose coins with an authentic look. Cleaning up a coin might lower its collector value by fifty percent or more.

Cleaning up coins resembles restoring artworks - they're both jobs ideally entrusted to specialists who have the understanding and experience to know when it's a good idea, what strategies are going to work best and how to utilize them appropriately.

If you do wish to undertake this effort, never ever abrasively clean coins. Even cleaning with a smooth fabric is going to cause little yet unwanted scratches, which are going to lower the coin's value.

If the surface of a coin seems tainted, it is best left alone. The color change is the outcome of a natural process, which collectors refer to as toning. Atoms on the surface of the coin have actually responded chemically, frequently with sulfur compounds. The response could not be reversed.

"Dips", which strip particles from the surface, are available. Dipping is the ideal example of a method that ought to be utilized just by experts, if at all. Furthermore, natural toning often increases the worth of a coin.

Dirt and other foreign substances sticking to a coin can often be taken out. You can try soaking the coin for a couple of days either in olive oil or soapy water, followed by a comprehensive rinse with tap water. Dry the coin with compressed air or permit it to air dry. Do not rub the coin. Professional coin cleaners might additionally be thoroughly utilized to loosen up foreign substances faster.

In case the coin has actually been cleaned with an abrasive, it is going to have hairlines. Likewise, abrasive cleaning frequently leaves some crud in the openings of the coin.

In case the coin has actually been dipped, it might or might not be noticeable. Although it is conceivable for an original coin to exist, it is not likely. Likewise, dipping can remove the luster off the coin.

A natural coin has a certain look which shows the history of its storage. Carelessly kept coins tend to have a "dirty" look to the toning. Coins that have actually lived for a number of years in a coin cabinet tend to have incredible colored toning.

Coins kept in a tidy metal vault (like an old-style "piggy" bank) might remain white (or red) for a number of years. Coins kept in albums establish either the familiar "ring toning" or the much less preferable "one-sided toning." Coins kept in mint bags frequently reveal incredible rainbow toning, comparable to that seen on coins kept in coin cabinets.

Copper/bronze/brass coins that have actually been cleaned have a strange color, frequently appearing like a toned gold coin. Even after they re-tone, they tend to be irregular and somewhat odd when it comes to color. Red in the recesses of that VF copper coin is normally not a great indication. Naturally toned, * circulated * copper tends to be extremely consistent in color, although they may be dark and filthy around the lettering and comparable protected spots. Un-circulated copper might tone extremely unevenly, so do not immediately count this against such a coin.

Just the other way around, silver coins that have actually been cleaned have a tendency to be exceptionally consistent in color after they re-tone, consisting of the tops of the letters and protected spots. Silver coins with natural toning are going to typically reveal some variation in the color at these areas. Understand that a uniform slate gray color could be produced on silver really quickly with a variety of chemicals. Lastly, a greatly toned and consequently dipped silver coin is going to tend to have a gray look brought on by surface roughness instead of a tarnish. This can be spotted by cautious assessment with a strong magnifier.

The ANA recommends that abrupt "hard-line" modifications in color do not take place on naturally toned coins. Naturally toned coins display a steady modification in color or darkness. Nevertheless, it's primarily a matter of looking at a great deal of coins and forming your own viewpoints. Presuming that you are purchasing coins for your individual collection, it is your opinion that actually matters.

Chapter 9: Grading Your Coins

Coin grading is a term utilized to describe the procedure of identifying the condition or quality of a coin. It is necessary to understand what the grade of a specific coin is, since the higher the grade, the higher its numismatic valuation.

Coins are usually graded on a 0-70 point scale created by Dr. William Shelby and recorded in the "Official ANA Grading Standards for United States Coins" book, released by the American Numismatic Association. Utilizing this approach of grading, the higher the point value, the better the shape.

The procedure of coin grading is more of an art than a science. While precise grading calls for ability and experience, figuring out an approximate grade is achievable for even a newbie coin collector.

The following qualities determine the coin's grade.

Mint State Perfect Uncirculated (MS-70).

This coin is a mint state un-circulated coin in ideal condition, reveals no traces of damage, blemishes, scrapes, handling or contact with other coins. This is the greatest quality of coin conceivable.

Choice Uncirculated (MS-65).

An above typical un-circulated coin that maintains all of the initial mint luster or appeal, however has a couple of contact marks on the surface or rim which are hardly visible.

Un-circulated (MS-60).

An un-circulated coin without any traces of damage, yet has a couple of contact marks, surface spotting or is short of its original radiance.

Choice About Uncirculated (AU-55).

This coin has really light wear on just the highest points of the layout, yet no other flaws and the majority of its luster continues to be.

About Un-circulated (AU-50).

The coin has proof of light wear on a number of the high points yet at least half of the mint radiance is still present.

Extremely Fine (EF-40).

The coin layout is lightly used in a lot of locations. However, all the attributes stay sharp and well specified.

Very Fine (VF-20).

Slight attributes such as a few of the finer hair details, feathers, and so on are going to be reasonably worn. Reveals moderate wear on peaks of the layout. All significant details are clear.

Fine (F-12).

Moderate to substantial even wear over the majority of attributes and the lettering. A great deal of the details are worn through yet you can still observe a significant amount of the design.

Very Good (VG-8).

The whole design is weak, yet a couple of details are apparent. Well worn throughout, however, coin rims are still apparent.

Good (G-4).

The coin is greatly worn; however, layout and legend are still noticeable, but rather weak in areas. Numerous details are gone.

About Good (AG-3).

This coin is extremely heavily worn with parts of lettering, date and legends worn hardly recognizable.

When there are substantial differences in between the obverse and reverse sides, a split grade might be appointed. Split grades are represented with a "/". For instance, "F/VF" suggests that the obverse is F and the reverse is VF.

The complete grade is typically determined by the obverse. An intermediate value might be suitable when the difference is substantial, particularly if the reverse is lower. A coin graded MS-60/ 61 would be considered to have a general grade of MS-60 and another at MS-65/ 63 might be considered to have a general grade of MS-64. Grade is just a part of figuring out a coin's value. Other aspects do enter into play.

Chapter 10: Figuring Out Your Coin's Value

Clearly, a coin will never ever be worth beneath its face value. A one-cent coin will never ever be worth less than a cent, nevertheless, it may be worth a lot more. Even if a coin isn't very valuable, it does not indicate it does not have a place in your collection. Just like with many things, the value frequently increases gradually.

The value of a specific coin is identified mainly by the following 4 elements:

1. Scarcity is a really essential element and has little to do with the age of the coin. Lots of one thousand-year-old Chinese coins typically sell for no more than a couple of dollars since there are a great deal of them around, whereas a 1913 Liberty Head Nickel might sell for over $1,000,000, due to the fact that there are just five recognized specimens out there.

2. The condition or grade of the coin is going to affect its value. An un-circulated coin in perfect mint condition may be worth thousands of times more than the identical coin in good condition.

3. Numerous coins have a bullion value figured out by the precious metals it consists of. A gold, silver or platinum coin does not typically sell for much less than its melt value.

4. The demand for a specific coin is going to likewise significantly affect its value. Some coins that are fairly numerous might command higher prices than scarcer coins, since they are more prominent with collectors.

For instance, there are over 400,000 1916D dimes out there as compared to just about 30,000 1798 dimes. Nevertheless, although the 1798 dime is much rarer than its 1916D equivalent, the 1916D coin sells for substantially more. The reason is, a lot more individuals collect early 20th century mercury dimes than dimes from the 1700s.

When you have actually figured out the grade, you can examine your reference book or any other publication to get the basic value provided to specific coins by professionals in the field. These are going to be the rough retail selling prices.

Coin prices are a feature of supply and demand. Market prices decrease when inventories can not be moved at present levels and ultimately increase when inadequate amounts are offered to satisfy existing demand. Naturally, if the purchaser or seller is uninformed of present trends, a transaction might take place outside the typical price range.

Dealers are going to typically pay less than wholesale when purchasing coins from the general public. For that reason, collectors and investors ought to understand that it is tough to "get their money back," should the need emerge to sell their holdings.

A credible dealer will ensure the genuineness of the product. He or she will be well-informed enough to form realistic viewpoints on grades, to find issues that might be missed out on by less knowledgeable collectors and will typically want to share knowledge with the general public, specifically customers.

Just because a coin has a particular value designated to it, does not always suggest that's what you can expect to get if you offer it, specifically if you offer it on e-bay.

On the other side, you might have a coin that individuals go bananas for. That's why e-bay is such a popular market for collectors. You can discover good deals for your collection online, and offer parts of your collection.

Chapter 11: Pricing Coins

A coin's value could be subjective. Generally, a coin is "worth" what somebody wants to pay for it. There are, nevertheless, basic rules for pricing your coins.

Identification: What nation released the coin? What is the face value, the date and the mintmark, if any? If more than one style was utilized that year, which one is it? Generally, this information could be figured out without much problem. Keep in mind that if no denomination is suggested, your coin-like item is, most likely a token or medal.

Authenticity: Fakes and modifications of lots of coins have actually been made by unethical individuals aiming to make a quick buck. A professional opinion might be required to figure out whether a coin is genuine.

Grade: A grade sums up the general condition of a coin. Fair market value typically differs by orders of magnitude for the identical coin in different grades.

Cleaning and other damage: Generally, collectors choose coins which have actually not been tampered with by cleansing or polishing. A coin that is worn away, scraped, holed, drilled through so that it could be held on a chain, changed, synthetically toned, "dinged" on the edge, or just unappealing for the grade is less preferable than a problem-free specimen. "Problem coins" are still bought and sold, however, usually at a significant discount rate compared to problem-free instances.

Grade and damage might have little or no impact on prices of coins which have a minimal numismatic value yet frequently lead to significant price differences for coins of interest to enthusiasts.

You can discover online price guides for U.S. coins at numismedia.com, however they note their prices at the upper end of the retail scale, so you can anticipate to get less than what they note.

Chapter 12: The Majority Of Requested Coin Values

Circulated U.S. Wheat Cents (1958 and earlier)

Many dated 1940 or later are bought by dealers for less than 2 cents each. A few of the earlier dates are worth more (a couple of cents to numerous dollars), and examining a price guide is a great idea in case you have them.

The existing design substituted the wheat stalk reverse in 1959. A handful of wheat cents are rather limited and command large amounts of cash. This style was initially utilized in 1909. Any cents of this vintage, in good condition, are worth numerous dollars. A few of the rarer 1909 varieties, are worth hundreds, in some cases 1000s of dollars.

There are additional scarce dates in the series, as well. 1932 cents and a few of the The Second World War error coins are likewise worth considerable sums.

1943 "Steel Cents"

Zinc-plated steel cents were minted just in 1943. A syndicated radio program improperly disclosed in early 1999 that these coins are scarce and precious. Actually, more than one billion were minted. What is scarce and precious is a 1943 cent struck on a regular bronze planchet.

Any 1943 cent that seems bronze must be evaluated to figure out if it's drawn to a magnet. In case it is, it's a steel cent that has actually been copper plated. Steel 1943 cents, might be worth less than 5 cents. Steel cents that have actually been "re-processed" and provided a brand-new zinc layer are not worth un-circulated prices.

Silver Dimes, Quarters and Halves

U.S. dimes, quarters and half dollars dated 1964 or earlier are 90% silver and were produced with 0.723 ounces of silver for every dollar in face value. As some metal might have been worn off from circulation, 0.715 ounce/dollar is typically utilized to approximate the quantity of silver still present.

Even if the coin is a common date, it's still deserving of more than face value due to its silver material. The quantity differs with the area price of silver.

Precious metal area prices are provided at Kitco Inc. Multiply the existing spot price of silver by 0.715 and by the overall face value. For instance, if the area is $4.00 per ounce, the bullion value for $100 face value is $ 4.00 x. 715 x 100 = $286.

Lots of un-circulated silver coins and some circulated ones might bring in a premium over the silver value. Look at a price guide to observe if you have any better dates. U.S. half dollars from 1965 to 1970 are 40% silver.

Silver Dollars

U.S. silver dollars from 1935 and earlier were created with 0.77 ounces of silver. These coins are prominent with collectors and can usually be sold for beyond their silver value. Less typical dates and higher grades could be sold for substantially more.

Susan B. Anthony Dollars

If you got it as a change, it's probably worth one dollar. Proof SBA dollars are worth more, however, proof coins are seldom discovered in circulation.

Bicentennial Quarters, Halves and Dollars

Since billions of these coins were made, they're usually worth just face value. A couple of dealers pay about 10% over face for rolls of lightly circulated bicentennial coins and a tad more for un-circulated ones. Special 40% silver bicentennial coins were additionally minted for sale to enthusiasts. They're quickly identified by the lack of copper on the brink. They're worth more than face value, yet are not likely to be discovered in circulation.

Coin Honoring the Wedding Event of Prince Charles and Princess Diana

Millions were produced by a number of British Commonwealth countries. The present price range for them is $5-25.

A Coin with 2 Heads, 2 Tails or Mules

With a couple of exceptions, these pieces are novelty objects often referred to as magician's coins. They're developed by burrowing one coin and trimming another to fit within. A seam can be discovered along the interior edge of the rim on one side. Since they're modified coins, they have no value to coin enthusiasts.

Nevertheless, a small number of genuine error coins called "mules" were found in 2000. A mule is created when dies meant for various denominations are matched to strike the two sides of a coin. The recently found mules consist of:

o At least one 1999 Lincoln penny with the reverse of a Roosevelt dime

o At least 6 Sacagawea "golden dollars" with the obverse depicting George Washington, meant for a state quarter

o A single Indian penny struck by 2 obverse dies, both dated 1869

In case you possess one of these extremely uncommon coins, a collector or dealer in your location might have the ability to help you in identifying if it's real. As soon as expertly verified, you might consign the coin at auction to get the best price.

An Un-struck Coin

Un-struck blanks or planchets are reasonably common. Many retail for a handful of dollars or less.

A "Mis-struck" Coin

There are numerous kinds of striking mistakes. In addition, a great deal of coins look uncommon due to the fact that they have actually been modified after striking. Modified coins have no value to coin enthusiasts.

Prices for genuine striking mistakes cover a wide range. Small mistakes, such as a raised fracture, will usually bring little or no premium. Unfinished planchets, referred to as clips, and off-center strikes normally sell for a couple of dollars.

Uncommon, remarkable mistakes might sell for many hundred dollars. The initial step towards figuring out the worth of an uncommon looking coin is to have it analyzed by several experts.

Chapter 13: Pricey Coins

The 1804 Silver Dollar, is the King of Coins. Just 15 exist and they remain in excellent condition.

The 1907 ultra-high relief $20 gold piece is thought about by many to be the most wonderful coin ever created. It was developed by sculptor Augustus St. Gaudens, and they're exceptionally scarce.

The 1913 Liberty Nickel is among the most popular coins on the planet. Thanks to its extreme scarcity and a publicity campaign by one of the industry's excellent marketers, B. Max Mehl. It's assumed the 5 coins were created unlawfully but the government has actually made no effort to seize them, which additionally brings in mystery to story.

By contrast, the 1933 $20 gold piece, which presently maintains the record for the highest price paid at auction, is a coin that has actually been diligently hunted down and seized by the FBI. The only piece that tops this chart is the sole example enabled to exist by the government, as the rest were purchased to be melted down by FDR in 1933. According to government records, none made it through, and considering that this is the official position, the Treasury imposes it.

The sole example was offered as a gift to King Farouk of Egypt, who was a devoted collector. Since its return to the world, following Farouk's death, the United States government has actually kept the position that it is legitimate, as it was a possession of foreign royalty as a present from the United States. The incredible sum commanded by this coin is due partially to its strange and appealing history and the possibility that it is going to stay one-of-a-kind.

The 1917 Type One Standing Liberty Quarter is among the genuinely wonderful U.S. coins. It was produced for just 2 years, since the exposed breast of Ms. Liberty triggered such outcry that they altered the design midway through 1917. Considering that the 1916 is a five-figure rarity, this coin is effectively a one-year-only type of coin. It makes the scarce coin catalog because of its collective allure, appeal, significance and top shape.

From 1795 to 1834, the U.S. minted $2.50, $5, and $10 gold coins. In 1834, the gold material of our coins was reduced somewhat and most pre-1835 gold coins struck the melting pot. Right now, these early treasures of American monetary history are scarce in all grades and incredibly scarce in Gem condition.

Today the Mint strikes countless proof coins a year and offers them to collectors throughout the world. In the 19th Century, the Mint struck a couple of thousand proof coins every year and just a handful of proof gold coins. Proof gold coins are the delicacy of the numismatic market. They are pricey, however they are incredibly scarce and demand is constantly sky high in both excellent and bad markets.

Barber Half Dollars were minted in between 1892 and 1915. They are among the coin market's most vital issues. They are gathered both by "date" and by "type" collectors and are the rarest of the 20th Century sliver type issues.

Twenty-Cent Pieces were odd coins produced for merely 4 years from 1875 to 1878. The coin appeared too much like a quarter to catch on with everyone and there truly wasn't a commercial requirement for the denomination. Right now, twenty-cent pieces are extremely treasured collector's objects.

Chapter 14: Kids And Coin Collecting

Numerous kids begin by picking up a coin they have actually never ever seen prior and continue collecting. Due to the fact that coin collecting necessitates very few tools, it makes an excellent pastime for a kid to begin and bring with them throughout their life. Kids of any age can acquire knowledge from these small pieces of metal.

They Can Boost Their Reading Capability

Many basic references on coins are written in relatively basic English, so kids can quickly comprehend the information. A lot of kids boost their reading capability when reading ends up being personally significant to them.

It is Going to Boost Their Understanding.

Coin collecting has a specific vocabulary. Even at the entry level, the collector needs to keep in mind lots of specific terms. The second a kid recognizes information is essential, they are going to discover a method to remember it.

They Can Refine Their Organizational Abilities

Coin collectors are constantly examining references, catalogues and information provided on the Web. The collector needs to be arranged, as information needs to be easily accessible and kept up to date.

They Establish an Interest in History and Culture.

You can not collect coins without finding out about individuals who produced them. Even if a kid does not continue with the pastime, they are going to be exposed to numerous other intriguing topics and establish an admiration for their value.

The Capability to Set and Reach Goals

Coin collectors are constantly making short and long term strategies. Couple of collectors are satisfied to have a casual array of coins. There is a good reason why each coin is included in the collection. Coin collectors wish to establish sets and obtain specific essential coins. Finishing a set of coins, even a little one, is viewed as a crucial achievement. The collector acquires a great deal of fulfillment from achieving goals.

It Develops Self-confidence.

Maybe the best reward that coin collecting provides young folks is the chance to legitimately take part in the adult world. There are no age limitations and there are a variety of teens who quickly ended up being well-informed numismatists. Knowing about coins is understanding that is valued by grownups and kids can find themselves in a role to teach and inform grownups about the pastime. Frequently, little success can turn into a great deal of ambition.

They are Going to Need to Develop Priorities

Figuring out priorities is frequently challenging for kids. There is a lot going on and typically their time and activities are planned for them. When it is their turn to choose what to do with their time, they frequently end up being bored. Coin collecting could be a really amazing pastime.

Value.

A typical grievance amongst adults is that kids do not comprehend the value of cash. The second they have cash, they spend it. A young coin collector should learn to save for that unique coin. They might be urged to consider ways to make additional cash by improving grades in school, working around the house, babysitting, or mowing the neighbor's lawn.

Getting A Kid Started

Coin collecting isn't for everybody. It takes persistence, time, and an interest before the seed could be sown. Nevertheless, revealing your own love for the pastime is the primary step towards getting youngsters included.

My great-grandfather, grandfather, and father were/are all passionate stamp collectors. When I was ten years old, my dad offered me my initial stamp album and some starter stamps.

For some time, I was the supreme stamp collector. My young life focused on discovering that evasive Queen Elizabeth purple cover, or purchasing a mixed bag envelope promoted in the back of my comics. Time stops me from continuing this pastime, however, I still like stamps and value what it has actually taught me throughout the years.

A little exposure to the pastime is typically all it requires to ignite an interest. If your household has actually saved a couple of old and possibly curious coins, you currently have the "starter set."

If your kid is interested and you do not have any old coins to begin a collection, go to a coin collector's store. A perfect option would be a collection of coins minted in the kid's birth year.

Conclusion

Folks gather coins for numerous reasons. Some collect due to the fact that they find the historic nature of the pastime really intriguing. Each coin is a real piece of the daily life of individuals who lived decades, even centuries back. These coins were used by the hands of countless individuals, a few of whom might even be individuals you've heard of.

A huge aspect of ending up being an effective coin collector is to study the subject and constantly discover brand-new information as it appears. Sign up with a local coin club in case there is one in your area.

Try to find coin collecting groups online. This can be a significant networking chance for you and the opportunity to discover somebody who has a coin you desire. The more individuals you know who enjoy coin collecting, the more opportunities you are going to have to contribute to your collection and maybe make a bit of cash too.

I hope that you enjoyed reading through this book and that you have found it useful. If you want to share your thoughts on this book, you can do so by leaving a review on the Amazon page. Have a great rest of the day.

Printed in Great Britain
by Amazon